Whispers

Poetry

By: Lauren Moe

Edited by: Nathaniel Wolfe

Whispers

Copyright © 2021 by Lauren Moe

ISBN 978-0-578-25734-1

Printed in USA by 48HrBooks (www.48HrBooks.com)

DEDICATION

I dedicate this book to the ones that believed in me and encouraged me to publish my poetry. They are the ones who have made this possible. You know who you are.

I dedicate this book to my path of victory and freedom. To my fervent prayers of faith for never giving up until I reached the other side.

There's a lot behind a photograph. For me, this path meant many walks and very long bike rides. It meant inspiration, my me time to clear my head and let the world speak to me in words. I've had so many ideas and thoughts going through my head walking on this path. It's where some of these poems came from. But, most of all, this bridge is the biggest part of "me" it represents my "trappings in life". I had to take the step to my freedom, and I had to get to the other side. I didn't just walk right through the bridge- There were ups and downs, and me- crawling, fighting, and not giving up until I reached it. And it was on one of those walks this bridge, though I walked through it so many times before, stuck out and *whispered* to me!

Job 11:16-18 (CEV) Your troubles will go away like water under a bridge, and your darkest night will be brighter than noon. You will find rest safe and secure, filled with hope and emptied of worry.

I am so happy to say that is my life now.

Most of all, I dedicate this book to My Lord and Savior Jesus Christ. He has given me this gift of writing, but best of all, saved me and set me free!

Table of Contents

Section 1:

Released through my redeemer

Section 2:

Whispers into life

Section 3:

Lost in love

Section 3:(continued)

Lost in love

Section 1

Released through my redeemer

Roar

I'm going to let the world hear me roar
no more holding back
it's time to soar
stop biting my tongue
when I've got God's word in my lungs

It's time to change
what the world hears
show them how I glitter
they can have awesome faith
and stop being a fence sitter
when God calls us all for more
it's time to start swimming
instead of just being on the shore

We can go so much deeper
we can stand out and shine
when we do what God has assigned
it's time for the world to see
his daughter of victory
the one that conquered
the daughter he set free

Doesn't even matter
if anyone wants to debate it
I will scream I will shout
`til the words he gives me come out
changing the lives
God wants to touch
I don't care if it's too much

The world is going to know
the name above every other name
when I bring the fire and the flame
so holy Spirit come
don't stop until your work is done!

Lightning bugs

Those nice quiet summer nights
when nothing is wrong
everything is feeling so right
kids running and laughing
not a care in the world

The dark sky now so clear
you see the lightning bugs appear
kids run to catch them
to put them in jars
while above you are a million
different stars

But if you sit,
and think about it,
if God can make a bug's butt
light up
just think of what else he can do
for nothing is impossible for you
if you just believe
the bible says it's yours to receive

So don't wish upon the stars above you
ask the creator who made them
tell him what you need him to do
so you can get your breakthrough

For even in the darkest of nights
those little bugs give us light
like a reminder of hope
that whatever you're going through
God's got you!

You thought you knew me

You thought you knew me
but so many years I would hide
behind these eyes
giving you a smile that was fake
while drowning in my tears
to fill a lake

Those nights crying in the tub
telling you I was just sad
I never told you that
it was all the alcohol I had

Bursting at the seam
not knowing
if you would judge me
and be mean

You never had a clue
so it was just so easy
I was so good at hiding
though it made me uneasy
I almost turned it into a game
but you seeking
that never came
I even wanted to get caught
but that I never got
so I'm sorry I didn't tell you
about all the alcohol I bought
the binge drinking I did
all the drinking from you I hid

I didn't tell you I had a problem
because I wanted to do it on my own
I told God that he and I could do it alone
and that's just what I did
God has set me free
and now he uses me
to tell others that
they too can be!

A mind of an addict

I have the mind of an addict
I don't think first before I act
I say what I want to
I don't care
even if it hurts you

I have a mind of an addict
one day I love my addiction
the next I wonder what I'm missin'

I have the mind of an addict
wanting so badly to be sober
but then not caring
knowing that my life is already over
I don't care that it's killing me
or it's destroyed my family
I'll do whatever to get my fix
In the book
I will use all the oldest tricks

I have the mind of an addict
my heart is hard
I've pushed everyone away
I've told them "not today"
tomorrow I'll quit
only to fall deeper into the pit

I have the mind of an addict
I am full of anger
I am trying to fill this void
then someone told me
Jesus can and he will
he can be your heart's true fill

I have the mind of an addict
but now Jesus is my drug
he gave me his grace
filling me with his love

I have the mind of an addict
addicted to Jesus
because he took away my pain
my guilt and my shame
my anger is gone
I will never be the same

I have the mind of an addict
but I am addicted to what's right
Jesus is now in my life
this addiction I no longer have to fight
my mind is so free
my addiction is gone
except to the one who is living inside of me!

Break free

I want to break free but
this addiction entangles me
these chains are tight
I'm too weak to fight
these demons are real
so is the guilt I constantly feel

I know I wasn't born this way
I am made in his image
the cross has the final say
so why can't I surrender today

All the times I said I'd quit
and failed
I just seemed to fall deeper into the pit
more guilt and shame
was all that remained

Yet your mercy and grace
never left my side
all the times I shouted and cried
begging for freedom inside
your love never left me
your arms were open wide
waiting for me to surrender
yet that-
I have to decide

but this addiction entangles me
my chains are tight
I'm too weak to fight
God, can tonight be my night

Will you kill these demons that are real
will you take away my guilt and shame
this addiction will you heal?

Good-bye

Today I said goodbye
to the misconception and the lies
you're in your pretty bottles
and catching to my eyes

You went down so smooth
but with every sip
I fell deeper into your grip
I thought you made me happy
but only guilt did I feel
crying out to God
this addiction won't you heal

I heard all the lines and verses that you set free
but freedom felt so far away from me
my chains were heavy
I was bound
but I didn't give up
then one day my freedom was found

I walked away
I said goodbye
I haven't looked back
I've stayed on track
no longer bound
my future looking bright
as I walk in my freedom
day after day
and night after night!

Do you wish to be free

Do you wish to be free
do you feel like you will be bound
for all eternity
I did too
`til one day my answer was found
it was so easy
I realized Jesus already
said it was finished
so I surrendered,
my addiction diminished

He helped me fight my temptation
becoming my firm foundation
now nothing is impossible
I see so clearly now
Jesus was my answer
if you wanted to know how

You can do it too
he will break your chains for you
turning your life around
just open up the bible where
all your answers will be found

Get on your knees and pray
he listens to all you have to say
ask him to come into your heart
that's the first step
to your new start

It doesn't take much faith
only faith as small as a mustard seed
and you will come to realize
Jesus is all you ever need

So don't go through life bound
you can be free
Jesus is the way
for all eternity!

Overcame

I overcame
for every day
it's the devil I slay
he has no power over me
because God gave me his victory
I overcame
my addiction inside
thought I was forever trapped
then God showed me the
door was open wide
it was that door I walked out
no more chains
no more trying to hide
I overcame
what Satan tried to claim
I am God's child
with him I was reconciled
I am an overcomer
I overcame
with God all things are possible
you only have to say his name
every day I wake up free
Satan has no more power over me
I conquered
I overcame
my life has never been the same!

Ready for more

Last year I still had some doubt
I still had some fear
that maybe you'd come back
but it's oh so clear
that I am free as can be
addiction lost all power over me
I'm moving forward
looking straight ahead
nothing impossible
my wings are spread
ready for more
than I ever thought possible before
everything so beautiful and bright
now that I am walking in the light
I have no regret
because getting sober was
the best decision yet!

Bar

Sitting outside looking at the bar
thinking about how I got
three and a half years in so far
but all it can take
is one false mindset
to fill your life
again full of regret

But let me tell you about the one I met
his name is Jesus
he set me free
so now I just think about eternity
I no longer think about
my next drink
or how I can fill the void
life is so different
it's life enjoyed

It's simple things
it's not feeling bad or guilty
and waking up hungover
it's completely enjoying this life sober

God gave me another shot
this is my do-over
I tell you this side of the fence
makes a whole lot more sense
I've got a life full of purpose
no longer having to pretend on the surface
for God looked at me
saw I was worth it!

Now I've got a whole new mindset
`cause I'm sittin' outside looking at this bar
it's so easy now to turn around and
just get in my car

Social media

On Tik Tok
everyone wants the most followers
yet what do we really gain
maybe a short time of some fame

On Facebook
it's all about keeping in touch with your friend
but do you realize in the end
it's really Jesus who you will face
to see if you are in his book
so his friend request I would accept

Instagram and social Media
you don't need to be verified
if you have Jesus by your side
he is the only one you want to follow
and then share
so when you arrive in heaven
you can also see
your friends and family there

So you can post your video on youtube
send out a tweet
but in the end it only matters
that it's Jesus you meet!

Fire in my soul

Put a fire in my heart
blazing flame in my soul
let me hang on to it
never let go

Give me your fire
burn out selfish desire
let me be the light for all to see

Give me your passion
make me who
you create me to be

Let your word burn inside
that I may not keep it in
give it to others
so they can know
you love them; forgive sin

Give me your passion
keep it lasting
create in me a clean heart

God make me ready
for this new season to start
fan this flame
let me never be the same

Satan *whispers*

Satan whispers
those lies in your head
soon fill you with worry, doubt, and dread
Satan whispers
tells you who you are not
soon you believe it and you're not
who you thought

Satan whispers
things that aren't true
Satan whispers
you will never find your breakthrough
Satan whispers
you will never be free
those chains are so tight
you have no more energy to fight

Satan whispers
bringing up your past
it's in your head
like a t.v. broadcast

Satan whispers
you will never get well
Satan whispers
you're just doomed to hell
Satan whispers
you will always be depressed

Satan whispers
your sins aren't forgiven
even though
you just confessed

Satan whispers
you're not pretty
you're not enough
and life will always be tough

Satan whispers
who do you think you are
you don't deserve that
Satan whispers but really, it's just chit chat,
are you really going to let him make you a door mat?

You need to let Jesus
walk in your head because
here are the things
Jesus would have said

My child I whisper all things that are true
you have my grace and hope
do you know how much I love you
you are the apple of my eye
I save every tear that you cry

You don't have to worry or fear
I am your Prince of Peace
I am always here

You are beautiful
fearfully and wonderfully made
you don't have to be bound or enslaved
for I call you free
so free you can be
for I give you my victory

You are more than a conqueror
for your battles I fight
day and night
I never slumber or sleep
so together those battles
we will defeat

I am your strength
I give you joy
you have my power so
Satan's works you can destroy

You are forgiven of all your sins
redeemed through my blood
so you gain eternity up above

When you confess,
I forget your sins as far as the east is from the west
your past is not your identity
it was crucified when your old life died

So child,
refute the lies that are in your head
don't listen to the stranger's voice
but my voice
the one whose blood for you was shed

You are the head and not the tail
you're my child and will never fail
I am the resurrection and the life
I give you streams of living water
your life is clay and I am the potter
whatever you do will prosper

I give you wells you did not dig
vineyards you did not plant
lands you did not toil
houses you did not build
all things spoken over you will be fulfilled

I have cattle on a thousand hills
I tell the winds and waves to be still
when you get a report
I have the final say
for I am the truth the life and the way

I can open any prison door
if you're weak and tired
you shall mount up with the eagles and soar
I created the heavens and the earth
what I've placed inside you
you will birth
my streets are paved in Gold
I shall renew your life
sustaining you when you are old
nothing is impossible through me
if you just believe
ask me
what you need and you will receive
I have good things planned for you
for I will see it through
these are the whispers that I Jesus have for you.

Eternity

Someday people will see
heaven and hell are real
so is eternity

Come to Jesus
he will show you the way
all you have to do is believe and pray

Turn from your sin
look into your heart
ask him to come in

He can set you free
heal your disease
nothing is impossible
if you just believe

He will be your provider
fill that void in your heart
he will be your Prince of Peace
and you-
his work of art

He will mold you
into the person you're meant to be
you can do anything
you will see

Have some faith
know he is the way
don't waste time
just do it today!

Section 2

Whispers into life

Purpose

Oh God show me what to do
what's your purpose and plan for me
reveal yourself
so my destiny I can see

I wanna hear your voice
seek your face
I hunger and thirst for your grace

All day long
my hope is in you
I know there's so much
you want me to do

But what is it
oh God
what is your plan
am I to finish what you began?

There's so much inside
I know I can give
everyday of my life
it's for you I will live

I just wanna know
but I wait on you
`cause I know in your timing
you will always come through

Time

When you're a kid
and you're in class
you can't wait for that bell to ring
soon enough it's Christmas
then it's spring

Summers leave without a trace
the tan on your face
quickly fades
as the leaves begin to fall
and all that's left is to remember it all

But it's funny
when you're young
time goes by so slowly
it's living off of mac and cheese
and canned ravioli
it's a "I can't wait for this"
"I can't wait for that"
wishing our time away
not realizing how fast
we will actually be older and gray

Then you graduate
maybe find your soulmate
time just keeps moving on
but now it feels like you blink
and another year's gone
now you are wondering –
where does the time go
looking at your kids
watching them grow

Camping trips, coffee dates, and vacations
turn into just trips down memory lane
but do you remember how long it felt
until you could actually board that plane

Counting down the days
once again in that phase
where time feels so slow
but you know
once you arrive
you will blink your eyes
and vacation's over

Time- it's like getting a puppy
the next thing you know
you're helping it cross the rainbow bridge
it's like already having to replace the fridge
thinking you just bought it
but you check the receipt date
and it's actually from 2008!

Time- it can just go so fast
so we have to make each moment last
time- it only gives us one life
so we should stop and smell the roses
we should still be thankful
when the door to that opportunity closes

`Cause when it is our time
this life will make sure we shine
take time to watch the sun set
finish this life without regret
like walking in forgiveness
saying your proper goodbyes
just once get up early
to watch the sunrise

Never giving up on your dreams
no matter how far away they seem
enjoy the small stuff
and the times when things get rough
for it's in those moments we grow
Time- it can be a crazy thing
it can feel fast or slow
but ultimately time is yours
you get to decide
how you will let time
be your guide

August

August comes
and there's a feeling in the air
like summer's ending
hardly feels fair
it's like it just began
thinking of snow and losing my tan
makes me dread
bitter winter ahead
kids get ready for back to school
pumpkin spice is soon all the hype
fall decorations starting to appear
it all becomes too clear
that soon,
winter will be roaring it's cold tune
and I will be back wishing for June

Camping

The smell of smoke in the air
as you set up your tent in the
perfect spot right there
so many things you can't wait to do
but the best is just being here with you

The hammock's in the tree
the sound of birds
has never made you feel so free
a short canoe trip in the water
the sun beating down
it's the feeling of being out of town

The nature around you
the critters astir
all the excitement
so the unwinding starts to occur

You start your fire
the warmth, the smell
the simplicity of all is well
roasting hot dogs and maybe a s'more
the sleeping under the stars
on the tent floor

Anticipating coffee in the morning
and breakfast in a cast iron skillet
can't you almost feel it?

This is camping
this is unwinding
this is about finding
the peace that being out
in nature can provide
so who wants to go camping
with me outside?

U-turn

I took a U-turn
the road down my past
chasing feelings
I wish would've last
trying to find that happiness
knowing it was real
wanting to once again feel

Memories from flashbacks
everyday round and round
like a train on the track
but since I can't go back
I wish these thoughts would derail
instead I keep remembering
every little detail
like when everything felt alive
when I looked at you
with a spark in my eyes

Now it's like I can't feel anything
just numb
waiting for relief in 2021
but will it ever really get better
will it get past "how you doing"
or talking about the weather
will I ever be able to say
that maybe I'm not ok
that I'm sick of hiding
that I've had enough
of all this covid stuff

Will the world ever come out of
the fear of the very oxygen they breathe
hiding behind this mask
does anyone know how long this is supposed to last?

We're told to stay home
only zoom with family
over the phone

Now I dream of get-togethers
with much warmer weather
a day that it's ok to hug
I dream of feeling a connection and love
summer nights with those Lightning bugs
counting the stars above
while twirling in the grass
knowing covid is now a thing of the past

But until this is reality
this U-turn takes me back
to a much better time
when memories provide
a feeling of happiness inside

Fork in the road

There's a fork in the road
don't take the path
you've always been told

Be brave and bold
the way that's right
may not be easy
but at the end of that
road there's light

You won't have to wonder
what's left
for the right path set you free
this right path
gave you your victory
this path allowed you to see
with eyes wide open
it was the right one chosen

If you will be brave
and you will admit
that you finally want to get out
of your pit

There's a fork in the road
with your story that's yet to be told
you must first be weak
so you can be strong
and reach out to say
it's time to move on

But now is the time
if it's out of that pit you want to climb
if you choose right
you no longer have to fight
you won't even have to look left
for your future you will re-write

There's a fork in the road
don't take the path you've always been told

Friends

What happens to friends
who say they're there until the end
only to drift apart
and are never there when
you need a heart to heart

Sometimes months go by
without even a text saying "hi"
neither side checks in
are we really that busy
even to ask "hey how've you been?"

Why do friendships fade
especially when they started out young
every day you went out and played
only to be separated by dinner and
having to go to sleep
now that friendship seems
so hard to keep

Did we really change that much
do a few miles, some kids, and marriage
really keep us from staying in touch
I wonder what the real reason is

Maybe we were only meant to be
for a season,
during childhood,
or whatever the reason

We all know friendships are hard to replace
so send that text and just say "hey"
it could end up being one
of the best things you do today!

Image

Inside my head
I see this perfect image of who
I would love to be
toned arms and ribs you can see
the perfect number on the scale
`cause in the mirror I only see
a beached whale
I only see my imperfections
my fat rolls and how I could be better
trying the latest diet or trend
only to feel guilty
I fell off of it over the weekend

Being bound to the scale
that tells you if today was ok
or a total fail
then trying to move on
to being ok with "healthy and strong"
instead of this number
in my head I see
that is lower than reality
then God reminded me....

I am fearfully and wonderfully made
I don't have to be bound
or enslaved
to this perfection
to this desire
that society seems to require
because in the end,
my destiny is heaven
and that, that is perfection

So while I am on this earth
I will open up the bible
and find my self worth
my identity is in him
not a scale
nor spending time at the gym

I am the apple of my fathers eye
so I don't have to compare
and listen to the lie
that I am not skinny enough
my body image is more than being buff
I will not let a number define me
when he already made me perfect
the way I was created to be!

Anxiety

I can't even enjoy a bike ride
I always have to beat the clock
when I walk
that has to be fast too
this anxiety
I just got used to

Never even thought about it
but now it's something
I must admit
when I sit
I'm not even still
I bite my nails and pick at my hands
for reasons I don't even understand
I fidget and think about
everything else I should be pursuing
like dishes and cleaning
and things I am not even seeing

Even at work
I am in a constant state of hurry
that my time there is just blurry
In my mind there is no rest
I pick myself apart
every time I get dressed

My thoughts consume
they even fill up the room
sometimes I can't let go
so they overwhelm my soul
my thoughts surround
some are heavy
I feel like I could drown

I'm just trying to find a way
to get this anxiety down
`cause even when I eat
my anxiety comes around
feeling guilty for what I just ate
worried that it might make me
gain weight

This anxiety I hate
but there will come a time
when I can unwind
and I'll forever be
free from this anxiety!

Dad

All I want is for you to be proud of me
but how can you be
if you've never been there

Life isn't always fair
but there was no reason
for you not to be a dad
you chose to be selfish and lazy
instead of raising your baby!

Don't you ever wonder what you did miss
and don't think to yourself "I already know"
because there's so much more to this

I forgave
and grudges I don't want to hold
but dad,
how can your heart be so cold?

I keep getting old
life slips away
you still never call
not even on my birthday

You say you love God
that you pray
I am not sure I believe that
`cause one day
you'll be gone

Will amends ever be made?

I wish with everything
that you would have stayed
my life I also wouldn't trade

I just wish you would at least try
but every time you do
it turns into a lie

So no more smiles will I fake
my heart
I'll no longer let you break
it's over and done
because into my life
I'll no longer let you come!

Paths

How come in life certain paths cross
only then to become lost
the path that led you to bliss
only turns into memories
and times to reminisce
dead ends or separate ways
or a path that only felt like a maze

Some paths you only get
for a season or a phase
and even though that's not fair
it was because it wasn't
going to lead anywhere

But we don't know that `til
we hit the dead end
or that fork in the road
when we have to decide
if staying on this path will
be worth the ride
or to just walk away and leave it behind
with the memories left in our mind

Maybe the path you are on now
feels like it leads to nowhere
but there is a path that leads to life
Just bow your head and say a prayer
if this is a path you haven't yet tried
I promise this path is worth the ride

So go ahead let Jesus be your guide
he will light up your path
weather narrow or wide
there won't be a fork in the
road or any dead ends
and to hop on
all you have to do is decide!

Behind these eyes

Behind these eyes
is a disguise
I may look happy
but my smile lies
`cause I'm really hurting inside
I can't shake it off
I just want to be left alone
to figure this out on my own

God feels so far away
I'm even struggling to pray

This season is a hard one
but I know the victory's already won
I just have to walk in it
so I am going to get up
I've had enough
Satan tried
but my faith is tough
I am stronger than all of this
I just have to agree
with the strength inside of me

I believe
with God there's nothing
I can't achieve

So I am shaking off the dust
with both feet on the ground
because I am going to turn
this season around

Morning Fog

Your life is like the morning fog—
it's here a little while
then it's gone
you don't know how many more
times you will see the dawn

When people on earth
are saying "rest in peace"
is God telling you "well done"
or maybe you don't know
if you will even meet his son

But if you're not dead
God's not done
you only get one shot
life doesn't give you a rerun

So what are you going to do
with the life he has given you
your time is short
and then we will stand before the Lord
so what is going to be in your report?

Truth is,
a lot of us don't think about the
day we will die
we think there's this day or that day
but shortly thereafter we're old and gray

We never did what God called us to do
we let the business of
life get in the way
some of us maybe just got lead astray

So here is your chance
what's in your heart
maybe your suppose to sing, write, or dance

But this is where you start
you ask Jesus into your heart
he will show you the way
he is the potter
you are the clay
you can walk into your true destiny today
so when the day comes
you can be confident you will meet his son
hearing those words
my servant, "well done"

Bicycle and me

It's just my bicycle and me
escaping from everyday reality
the sun shines, the birds sing
I'm not worried about anything

It's just my bicycle and me
miles and miles go by
the wind's in my face
that bicycle is my favorite place

It's just my bicycle and me
rain or shine
I'm thinking about biking all the time
`cause there's nothing we can't do
it's what I look forward to
there's no place we can't go
biking is my high
when I'm feeling low

No matter what bicycle it is
I'll pedal away any bad feelings
or thoughts that day

So it will always be my bicycle and me
forever
until I reach eternity!

Honor

A Purple Heart
a bronze star
doesn't even compare
to who you are
you are our hero
grandpa, father, and son
so we salute you for all you've done

With honor you fought for our land
noble and brave
for many lives you did save
with honor to the
red, white, and blue
we now want to honor you
a world War II vet
with honor
we'll never forget

You sacrificed
gave it your all
we are so proud
for you we stand tall

Your time came
you took God's hand
when you heard him call

So until that day when we meet again
we will honor you
grandpa, our hero,
with our heads held high

We say goodbye....

*For Robert W. Earl. Thank you for your service, your sacrifice, but most
of all, for saving my life! Miss you grandpa.

Memories

Memories
sometimes they are the best
sitting around a campfire talking about
that canoe trip where you caught that trout
or regretting the time you drank too much
and blacked out

Memories
some don't you wish
you could forget
like that time you lost way too
much money on a bet

Realizing memories would be easier if that person
you never would have met
since you can't go back and hit the reset
now there's a memory full of pain

See every choice we make
there's memories at stake
some will be good and some sad
some you will wish you never had
some will make you smile
around the campfire

Other memories you wish would retire
some can come with regret
while others are easy to admire

A memory
one that's never gone
you tell yourself today
will be the day I move on

I won't think about this
because it's just too hard to reminisce
but this memory doesn't skip a beat
everything they said is in
your head on repeat

The feelings a memory can give
can make you laugh
just like looking at an old photograph

Feelings are behind a memory
As you travel back in time
so choose wisely what you do
because those choices turn into
memories that will forever follow you!

Section 3

Lost in love

Lost

Did you get lost in me
like I got lost in you?
Now it's like we're in this maze
not knowing what to do
all the dead ends
twists and turns
one of us is bound to get burned
as much as we want it
and I love your charm and wit
we must admit
this will go nowhere
so it's not really fair
it's not worth the cost
to keep getting lost
it's just so hard
it only brings us down
so maybe it's best
if you stop coming around

Twirl me around

You pick me up and
twirl me around
got that look in your eye like;
"look what I found"

You're on for the chase
and I'm in love with your face
oh your green eyes
you're like a prize that I can't claim
so we "ring around the rosie"
but no one wins this game

We definitely ignited the flame
but you're not ready yet
so these feelings I really gotta tame

So we dance around each other
and we behave
but deep down I'd be your slave
I pretend you don't intoxicate me
as you push me away

But I can't help what I want
I want to make you happy
fulfill all that's inside
if only it were that easy
I would jump in and take a ride

Nervous

When I see you
I'll just have to fake it inside
that I'm not nervous
and everything just came alive

My heart is like a flower
it blooms when you're around
gotta keep myself together
and not break down

The feelings that I found
I'll just have to drown
pretend my heart isn't racing
tell myself not to be that puppy dog
after you it's always chasing

I just have to breathe
pray time stands still
tell myself to just
relax and chill
but with one line
you can take all this away
you always have
the perfect thing to say
to make me laugh or smile
forget about the nerves for a while

Except it's like you have this power over me
you draw me in like bait on a hook
everything's on fire
with just one look
so if you're standing by my side
I'll fake it that I'm not nervous
and a total wreck inside!

Blind

They say love is blind
and that is so true
`cause no matter what you do
I can't stop loving you
it doesn't matter what I've heard
or where you've been
I just want to love you `til the end
I don't know how much longer
I can be strong
but I also can't talk myself
out of moving on

Best friend

If I have to be your best friend
if that's all I get
then I'll take my job with honor
I'll be the best one yet

I'll offer you my shoulder
I'll show you that I care
I'll be there when you need me
I'm not going anywhere

If I have to be your best friend
the one that hears you cry
then I'll take my job with honor
I'll take my job with pride

My love for you is stronger
than you'll ever know
but for you to ever love me
I'll have to let you go

You need time to find your purpose
you need time to sort your thoughts
but when the course has ended
and the race is finally run
remember it's me, your friend,
who has loved you from day one!

In or out

You let me out
you let me in
I can no longer take this again
I have tried to help you
to make things better
but I always say everything wrong
so now I dunno where I belong
in your arms
or by your side
a lover or a friend
you can't decide
my flaws seem much too great
it's me you don't appreciate
it's off
it's on
I guess I can't clean up this mess
I thought we were going to progress
but only friends we are again
because of my past sin
no matter what I do
I can't seem to win
so tell me to stay away
or let me in
`cause I no longer know
I wanted these feelings
for each other to grow
but if it's easier I will go
I can leave
if it's friendship
we can only achieve
that's fine with me
I can no longer play this game
so whatever our relationship is
it's yours to name

Winter

This winter
I'll be loving you
when it's cold and we're blue
I'll keep you warm
the whole way through

This winter
I'll be loving you
I'll hold you tight
when we're on the futon
watching movies all night

This winter
I'll be loving you
through the storm
when it's below zero
this winter you'll be my hero

This winter
I'll be loving you
we'll laugh and play
making a snow angel some Saturday

This winter I'll be loving you
next winter too
in the spring, summer, and fall
I'll be loving you through it all

Disguised

Thank you
for getting me through
but your love
I wasn't expecting too
you took my hand
I looked in your eyes
I fell inside
my heart disguised

Sinking

I was tired and sinking
so I reached out and grabbed
you as my life line
now all that's left between us is time
but time with us just
never seems to align

We drifted apart out to sea
and what is left-
a piece of debris
a message in a bottle
full of memories this bottle does contain
with two hearts full of love
that will always remain

Some days I am drowning
thinking about it all
and being ok again
hiding behind my wall

When you see a bike or hear the rain
does it make you happy or does it bring you pain
sometimes I catch myself in a smile
other times it's easier
to bury it in one of my "files"

I will never fully heal
because it was all too real
but then time ran out
no more lifeline
so I'm just pretending I'm fine

It's crazy to think that such happiness can actually exist
and that's what I've most missed
it would be easier to drown in a sea of forgetfulness
that way it would hurt less

`Cause the memories I have
and the pain I feel
are just a constant reminder
it was all so real

But I gotta stay grounded on this shore
I gotta get ahold of my anchor
and like the butterflies
I need to fly free
I need to find that lifeline
that leads me
to true destiny

Fall

The leaves will fall
the season will change
sometimes feelings
will get rearranged
but the air is crisp
things feel new
just like every time
I get to see you
bad feelings fall away
like leaves on a windy day
I smile
my colors shining through
like the fall leaves get to
autumn air so chilly
but you warm my heart
you always have
even from the start
the crunch beneath my feet
as I walk on those fallen leaves
brings back last year and
all the memories
what a season we went through
but how good it was
that last fall you were sent
an angel from up above

Sweatshirt

It took me a long time
to wash that sweatshirt
then the day I did it really hurt
`cause the scent started to fade
just like the memories we made
putting it on made me feel so close to you
but that also is just a memory too

It's been so long
I didn't think I'd still be crying
over a break up song
but my love for you never washed away
I'm still trying to kill the part in me
that longs for you every single day
`cause it just felt like destiny
you and me

I must admit I miss you like crazy
you are in everything I see
obviously, even my laundry
but as your voice in my head
becomes an echo
and I struggle to find
ways to let go
I realize I don't even know
if you still think about me
so maybe the way I feel
is just wasted energy

but we were like paradise
a vacation everyday
so much happiness inside
it's heartbreaking you couldn't stay
so I put that sweatshirt on
when I'm thinking of you
because just like the static
it's still you that I'm clinging to!

Under your spell

You've got me under your spell
and boy I fell
I can't give you up
got me saying your name
oh what a dangerous game

I didn't see this coming
cupid hit me hard
so hard I let down my guard
I can't even get back up

I am completely paralyzed by you
and that arrow that cupid drew
I don't want the antidote
or the cure
I just want you

It's oh so clear
these feelings I can't tame
no stopping the fact
you drive me insane

When I hear your voice
it's like music to my brain
can't stop the rush
goes right to my heart
igniting a spark
electricity running through my veins
these feelings of love I cannot contain

Burning so hot
but I like it a lot
whatever spell you've got me under
it's totally working
so you don't have to wonder

Lullaby

Today I cried
the music that was on
sang me a sweet lullaby
memories flashed
right before my eyes
all the "how's" and "why's"
but especially the goodbyes
made me so sad
about all that we lost
when it was everything we had
that's what hurts so bad
time has kept moving on
but to you my heart is still drawn
nothing has changed
I'm still trying to heal
because I'll never get past
the way you made me feel

Fantasy

You get so lost in this fantasy
all these people are around
but all you see is me
like everything for you disappears
you have no worries and no fears

Yet here I am losing my mind
thinking about every little thing
all of the time
it's like you don't have a care
you just take me all in and stare

I love the way you love
it's just so real
something you cannot conceal
it's like I am this dainty little flower
you don't want to break
but stick in a vase
so you can constantly watch
and keep it safe

I just want to take it all in
make it last forever
but nothing this good lasts forever
especially when this storm we
constantly have to weather

Your eyes look into my soul and
I just know
how things could be
and for a moment,
it makes my heart happy

But for now,
I can be your dainty little flower
that you keep in a vase
inside your heart
to stare at and keep safe

Butterflies

Sometimes just thinking about you
takes my breath away
my heart will pound
and the butterflies
turn my stomach around
it's like you walked into my
heart
like you always belonged there

Meet me in the stars

I look up at the sky
and what do I see
a million stars waiting for
you and me

So meet me in the stars
where we can be together all night long
meet me in the stars
because together is where we belong

Meet me in the stars
nobody will be there
we can spend the day
talking it away
I'll take your hand as we
dance under the milky way

Meet me in the stars
and maybe for a bit I will let go
of all my worries that continue to grow

We can walk through the galaxies
wild and free
I'll be so happy with you just
next to me

So meet me in the stars
it's the perfect place
where we can embrace
up in outer space

Sail away

Come sail away with me
we can drift out to sea
no more worries
we can be free
you can hold me from behind
when we watch the sunset
to unwind
with the wind in our sails
we will not fail
so let it take us where it may
as long as we have each other
it will always be a happy day
we could stop at a beach
feeling the sand
beneath our feet
the warmth of the sun on our face
and your love's perfect embrace
so what do you say
do you want to sail away?

Official

Do you have any idea
how bad I want you
want you to make it official
that you're going to be
the one I'm with forever
I'd do anything
to have your last initial

`Cause I want you
every single night
to be with you
holding you tight

So marry me today
so I can be with you tonight
every day I want you so much more
to show you how much I love you
in a place of our own
so at night
I won't have to be alone

I want you to make it official
`cause I don't want any other man
I've given you my all
I want you to be the last

So many things I'll never say
wanting you in every single way
there's nothing I could buy
there's nothing I can do
to ever show you
how much I love you

In this world there's not enough money
there will never be enough "I love you honey"
not even a thousand hugs would be enough
or if every second I'd stop to give you a kiss
or if we took a vacation full of bliss
to show you my love
no material thing would ever exist

More than this world
I do love you so
you're all I think about
and I hope you know

You're all that I want
in every single way
I want to share my love
with you every single day

Oh make it official
`cause I know you're the one
I want to share my life
`til it's over and done

So marry me today
I can be with you tonight
because being with you everyday
will always feel right!

Obsession

I am his obsession
in his mind his possession
his eyes go where I go
completely transfixed
always wanting to know
images in his head
thinking of me
he dreams of what we could be
how things would go
how he and I would flow
I live inside his mind
and like a fine wine
he just wants a taste
all the time

You

You live in my mind
stamped in my heart
always with me
never apart
you light up my life
making things better
you make me feel cozy
like my favorite sweater
you look at me
like no one else does
it gets me so high
like the clouds above
you compliment me
say things I could
only dream of
you are the rain
unpredictable at best
but it keeps me on my toes
as this love continues to grow
you will continue to live in my mind
because my heart decided
I'm not letting go this time!

Will this last

Lying here watching time pass
I'm wondering
how long will this last

We caress each other
then we kiss
nothing has ever felt like this

You say things then I fall for you
we've been through all of this
we get so close then we drift
my heart being ripped out
then put back in
when I sit here holding you again
but to actually have you this time
I can't help but doubt

I look at your face
at the perfection of your outlines
you are so astonishingly fine
I want to tell you how badly
I want you to be mine
but we drift off in a sleep
and you smell so good
feeling so comfortable next to me
I would stay here all night if I could
I don't want to leave until there is closure

But we get in your car
kissing one last time
your lips feel so good
against mine

When you drive off
it makes me wonder
if falling for you
will be just like the past
or if this time
we will actually last!

Autumn day

That Autumn day
it was gloomy
except for that tree
displaying itself yellow
you also caught my eye
having me at "hello"
what a perfect scene
that felt like a dream

Pull me close

Pull me close
don't let me go
you're all the love I need to know

I want it more
as it continues to grow
there is no other that has made
me feel like this
so pull me close
I'll seal this love with a kiss

I've never wanted anything more than this
this love, these feelings
are all so real
so pull me close and I'll
tell you exactly how I feel

I daydream about life with you
how it would be-
so easy, so much love, and me being me
never wanting to leave your side
endless talks, holding hands,
watching sunsets outside

So pull me close
my arms are open wide
I'll hold you forever
until you're satisfied

Will you pull me close
and never let me go
I'll give you all my love
all the love from you
that I now know

Movie

Nothing feels real
it's like a dream
the way I feel
is it really this way
am I really all the things you say
could this love really be
like in the movies we see
can we really have
this much chemistry?

What about our connection
I can read you when you're
not even near
I can feel it
it's also in my head crystal clear
I get your vibes
I read your eyes
when we touch I feel your heart
and what's really inside
like your love for me you can't hide

I've tried but I can't let you go
I can't wake up from this dream
`cause I don't want to know
if this is real or how it all ends
maybe it's just the beginning
and we end up winning

But in order to know
we have to wait
for the second movie is coming
that will reveal our fate!

Wall

How did you just walk
right through my wall
I had my guard up
so you wouldn't fall
but the way you look at me now
says you want it all

To you I was just a kid
and behind that
wall I hid
`til you broke it down
and the real me was found

Then you saw a woman
with her soul on fire
it's easy to see
I'm what you admire

One day there was a click
it just happened so quick
your eyes said they loved me
now there's this energy
there is nothing you can say
your eyes said it all
the moment I watched you fall

I can feel the way you feel
you can never hide
I know this feeling has
been bottled up inside

Now both our souls are on fire
as our hearts did collide

Now I can't put my wall back up
`cause how do you undo
the connection that's so true?

So here's to you
that you don't even have to say it
that I've already known
the day you looked at me
like I was yours to own

Electricity

You don't even have to kiss me
for me to feel the electricity
you don't even have to be near
our energy could
light up a city

You don't even have to hold my hand
for my heart to understand
that you're meant to be my man

When you're on my mind
my heart jumps around
I need a defibrillator just to
calm me down
you shock all my insides
the volt is amplified
very hard to hide

You send a current
of love throughout
I realize it's you I can't live without

I bet we could start a fire
if we touch
of explosive fireworks
would it be too much?

Together our smallest spark
could light up the dark
kinda like you light up my life
and the stars above
you are everything I love

Our energy is so real
it's nothing we really can conceal
I can't control it
it's just how I feel
just so you know
you don't even have to be here
for this energy
to be extrasensory

Cabin

In my dream
you took me to
that cabin by the lake
I helped you cook
you watched me bake

In my dream
we watched the sunset
holding each other tight
you wouldn't let go of me all night
in the morning we watched the sunrise
though I am shy
I let you look me in the eyes

In my dream there were no goodbyes
we got to talk the day away
we laughed and we played
I listened to you scold me about
running barefoot in the grass
never thinking about
the time that had passed

I fished and you just
watched every little thing I did
smiling at me
acting like a kid
then you took my hand
led me back to bed

We just laid there
as I read the thoughts in your head
telling you about the things
you never said
then suddenly I woke
and I was in the wrong bed

Drown in your love

I want to drown in your love
there is nothing better I know of

I get so high
I'm on cloud nine
wishing you were mine

Let me swim
in your ocean of love
that's so far and so wide
it's getting harder to hide

You're always on my mind
constantly drifting out to sea
wanting to be with thee

Oh how I love you so
but It's not easy
since I don't know
if your feelings for me
ever grow

So I just hang out at the shore
hoping for more
that you'll pretend to be fishing
but you catching me instead
is what I'll be wishing

Cut me open

You cut me open with your eyes
they pierce me on the inside
leaving me so exposed
and open wide

You can see my soul
and you know
the flame that burns
below

My heart's on fire
burning with passionate desire

It rages inside
like the waves upon the sea
igniting my soul
driving me crazy

You've cut me deep
leaving me weak
as our spirit ignites the spark
you've awakened
my soul and captured my heart

Leaving me wanting more
so you see,
you cut me open with your eyes
and this is me on the inside.

Long lost love

I have a long lost love
but you're not really lost
you just need to be found

Maybe sometime in the future
I will find you
and you will find me
we won't be lost anymore
we will be as one
sailing out to sea

Drifting…..

Just you and me
our hearts complete
our souls finally free

Until then,
you are always in my heart
in my mind
in my soul
in my thoughts
and in my tears
every single year

The end

You made it to the end
my love and gratitude
to you I send

My wish is that you think about
lightning bugs and the stars above
you take your memories
hanging on to the ones
you most love

May you too follow your dreams
not allowing precious time to slip away
your morning fog
turning into a sunny day

May you hear the whispers of God
text that best friend
choose the right path
that hopefully doesn't lead
to a dead end

Find that true love
that at first makes you nervous
and always thank a vet for their
sacrifice and service

But most of all,
thank you reader,
for the time you took
to support my biggest dream
by reading this book

About the Author

Lauren Moe, author of Whispers

Lauren was born in San Diego, California and raised in Minnesota. She currently resides in Wisconsin with her husband, Lance. Lauren considers her faith and family to be most important to her. She loves to bake and enjoys outdoor adventures. If she isn't spending time in the gym, on her bike, hiking or running along the trails of the bluffs; you can almost always find her surrounded by her sweet dogs, Jack and Jill, and cats, Obi and Charlie. Lauren began journaling in fourth grade which lead to her love for writing poetry. She is very excited to share her heart with you in her first poetry book.

15